Sydney

a panoramic gift book

Steve Parish

Contents

5 Sydney

7 Sydney Harbour

15 Darling Harbour

21 The Opera House

29 The Bridge

33 Circular Quay

34 Sydney Tower

37 Taronga Park Zoo

39 The City

47 Southern Beaches

50 Northern Beaches

57 Blue Mountains

58 South Coast

60 Central Coast

Sydney

from the heart

Sydney, with a diverse, multicultural population of over four million people, is the largest city in Australia. The first Europeans to live in Australia settled in Sydney, and over time it has developed into one of the most vibrant and cosmopolitan cities in the world.

In Sydney, I am always aware of the waters of the harbour and the Pacific Ocean beyond. The ferries and pleasure craft making their way through the glittering waterways provide efficient transport and leisurely recreation. The beaches with their surf and sand are made for relaxing. It was the sea that first drew me to this city — I served aboard naval vessels anchored in the harbour and I spent my weekends scuba diving in its waters. These days, I wander Sydney's streets looking for images that capture the essence of this lively city by the sea.

Steve Parish

A luxury liner leaves Sydney Harbour on its way out of Sydney Cove. The Royal Botanic Gardens, Sydney city and the Opera House form a backdrop.

The *Bounty* replica has its mooring at Darling Harbour.

Sydney Harbour

the perfect port

Sydney is built around beautiful Port Jackson. When Governor Phillip arrived with the First Fleet in 1788, he found Botany Bay unsuitable for a settlement and investigated Port Jackson. He liked what he saw — a magnificent harbour that offered a haven for ships, a water supply at the head of Sydney Cove and a location where an isolated settlement would be safe from bombardment from the sea.

The rugged sandstone headlands that define the harbour are the visible remains of a drowned river valley. Unlike many estuaries, Sydney Harbour has its highest sandstone cliffs on the coast.

Sydney has always been a port. Its deep water provides an excellent berth for the world's largest ocean liners, commercial cargo traders and container ships.

Looking north-east from Potts Point and Kings Cross over Rushcutters Bay, with Clark and Shark Islands on the left in the middle distance.

Rushcutters Bay is home to the Cruising Yacht Club of Australia. Beyond it lie Double Bay and Rose Bay.

Sydneysiders are passionate about sailing.

Above, left to right: North and South Heads; Mosman Bay; Gladesville Bridge over the Parramatta River.

Above, left to right: The Spit, Middle Harbour; Felix Bay, Point Piper; looking across The Gap to Watsons Bay and the city.

Circular Quay by night.

The Sydney Harbour Bridge illuminated after dark.

The Opera House glows white under evening lights.

The *South Steyne*, a retired ferry employed as a floating restaurant, docked at Darling Harbour.

Darling Harbour

waterfront leisure centre

Darling Harbour was originally called Cockle Bay. Here the Aboriginal clan, the Wangals (part of the Eora tribe) used to forage for shellfish.

The Darling Harbour complex was once a railway goods yard. An imaginative plan sought to convert this area into the shopping and recreational complex we see today. The task became a bicentenary project and the complex was opened in 1988, two hundred years after the arrival of the First Fleet.

Darling Harbour is in easy walking distance of the city. Otherwise it can be reached on the monorail, on a ferry from Circular Quay, or on a tram, which now runs from Central Station, passing close by Darling Harbour as it travels to the Sydney Fish Markets and the inner-city suburb of Lilyfield.

Cockle Bay Wharf, Darling Harbour, is a fine place for a stroll in the Sydney sunshine.

Pedestrians and the monorail use the old Pyrmont Bridge to cross Darling Harbour.

In the Sydney Aquarium, visitors follow a tunnel through the massive feature tanks.

Promising entertainment galore, Darling Harbour is a locus for family fun. Activities include Sydney Aquarium and Wildlife World.

International Code of Signals flags outside the Australian Maritime Museum.

Looking east at the Opera House on Bennelong Point.   Pages 22–23: The Opera House and Harbour Bridge seen from Mrs Macquaries Chair.

The Opera House

inspired architecture

The Sydney Opera House was designed in 1956 by the Danish architect Jørn Utzon.

The Utzon design envisaged auditoriums that would be protected by giant shells rising like sails above the base of the building and the harbour. (These distinctive "sails" are clad in tiles of white granite.) The building was not designed to have an apron — it was to look as if it were floating.

The Sydney Opera House was finally finished in 1973 and opened by Queen Elizabeth II on 20 October, even though the first commercial production took place in the Opera Theatre on 28 September. The performance was of the Australian Opera's production of Prokofiev's *War and Peace*.

One of the shells closed off with tinted glass, viewed from the forecourt.

The majestic Opera House, stark white against the brilliant blue of the sky, as seen from Farm Cove.

The grand interior of the Concert Hall.

As darkness envelops, the silhouettes and shadows are quite mystical.

From any perspective, the Opera House always makes a bold statement.

The steps leading from the forecourt to the performance areas.

The bridge's arch rewards climbers with a stunning vantage.

The Bridge

the harbour's beloved "coathanger"

The Sydney Harbour Bridge was a triumph of the Great Depression, designed by John Bradfield and built by an English company, Dorman Long.

The arch was built in two halves. Each half was supported by huge steel cables that were anchored into U-shaped tunnels dug into the sandstone base rock. The top and bottom curves of the arch were constructed using creeper cranes.

After the arch was complete, the deck was started. Work on the deck began at the centre of the bridge and moved outwards.

On Saturday 19 March 1932, the Sydney Harbour Bridge was officially opened by the New South Wales Premier, Jack Lang.

A twilight view west from Mrs Macquaries Point to the Opera House and the Sydney Harbour Bridge.

A Manly ferry makes its way from Circular Quay around Bennelong Point.

Circular Quay

birthplace of a nation

On 26 January 1788, the first British settlement in Australia was founded by Governor Arthur Phillip on an inlet named Sydney Cove. Phillip was the commander of the First Fleet that left England on 13 May 1787. The Aboriginal name for the area around Sydney Cove was *Warran* or *Werrong*.

Almost immediately, the Sydney Cove area developed as a port. In 1835, work began to build a sea wall around the cove and reclaim the mudflats behind the southern end of the wall. This reclaimed land was shaped like a horseshoe and was known as Semi-Circular Quay. The "semi" eventually dropped off and the area is now known as Circular Quay.

Early in the 20th century, the sea wall was gradually straightened to form a rectangular area.

Sydney Tower

a stellar vantage

Sydney Tower presides over the Centrepoint Shopping Centre and, at 305 metres, is the tallest building in Sydney. The tower consists of a shaft of steel and barrel-type units surrounded with external cables that strengthen the structure. On top of this is a four-storey turret that is connected to the ground by high-speed lifts and two stairways. An à la carte revolving restaurant is on the first level of the turret, and a revolving restaurant with a buffet-style menu is on level 2. Level 3 is a function room and coffee lounge, while an observation deck is on level 4. On top of the turret is a 162 000 litre water tank — this dampens vibration in the tower as well as providing water for the sprinkler system should there be a fire. A 31-metre spire extends from the top of the turret; communication antennas are attached to it.

Sydney Tower and the monorail that runs clockwise around the city centre.

The top of Sydney Tower offers 360 degree views of the city.

Taronga Zoo's famous Neo-classical lower entrance.

The giraffes at Taronga Park enjoy a multi-million-dollar view.

Taronga Park Zoo

prestige haven for wildlife

Taronga Park Zoological Gardens were established at the present site in 1916. The zoo was previously located on a site near the Sydney Cricket Ground that is now occupied by Sydney Girls High School.

The steeply sloping site can be entered from Taronga Wharf on Sydney Harbour. From there, a chairlift or bus will carry visitors to the top. When going through the zoo, it is always better to start at the top and walk downhill!

The zoo has a wonderful, creatively displayed, collection of native and exotic animals. As well as sharing these fascinating creatures with the public, the Taronga Park Zoo is part of a worldwide conservation program that aims at saving endangered species from extinction.

This bright mural adorns Oxford Street in Paddington.

The City

the hub and heartbeat

Sydney offers so much. For fine Asian food and shopping, head to Chinatown. For bars and night life, try Kings Cross. If you want to see a film, odds are that it will be showing in a cinema on George Street. For shopping, art galleries and good coffee, try Paddington, Glebe or Surry Hills. If the business world is your mecca, you'll find financial institutions from Martin Place to the Quay. For live performances, the Opera House or the Town Hall stage cultural theatrics. Visit the Australian Museum or the Museum of Sydney to learn more about this wondrous land. And, if you want a quiet place in which to reflect, go to one of the great cathedrals — St Andrew's near the Town Hall or St Mary's near the Australian Museum.

The Australian Museum, opened in 1827, is the country's oldest museum.

The grand organ in Centennial Hall, the auditorium of Sydney Town Hall.

Looking down the nave of St Mary's Cathedral to the high altar and chancel.

Queen Victoria's statue silhouetted against the Sydney Town Hall.

Looking down George Street towards Circular Quay past the Queen Victoria Building.

The *Great Australian Clock*, designed and made by Chris Cook, is inside the Queen Victoria Building.

George Street North, The Rocks.

The Coca Cola sign has become a Kings Cross landmark.

The Royal Botanic Gardens and the Domain wrap around Farm Cove.

Dixon Street, Chinatown.

Governor Arthur Phillip fountain.

Looking over Bondi Beach and the eastern suburbs to the distant city centre.

Southern Beaches

classic summer escapes

Bondi is one of the world's most famous beaches. It has a very deep apron of sand and a great surf break. Like all of Sydney's beaches, Bondi is manned by professional lifeguards and amateur lifesavers. It is compulsory to swim between the flags and bathers can be fined for ignoring this rule.

Each beach in the eastern suburbs has its own particular following. Each has something that makes it special. All of them are closely guarded by the mighty sandstone cliffs that define the coastline. All have marvellous rock platforms that support rich and varied marine life. And all of them can easily be reached by public transport.

Coogee Beach, one of the smaller and more intimate beaches.

Maroubra Beach, considered one of Sydney's best surfing beaches.

Looking north along Bondi Beach, Australia's most well-known beach.

Bronte Beach in Nelson Bay has tidal baths built in the southern rocks.

Tamarama Bay is a beautiful spot just north of Bronte.

Northern Beaches

where style meets surf

The northern beaches start at Manly and extend as far north as Palm Beach. Manly was named by Governor Phillip because of the manly disposition of the Aboriginal people he met there during his first visit to the area in 1788. Manly was also the beach on which, in 1902, William Gocher successfully contested the ban on recreational bathing during daylight hours.

Most of the northern beaches are long, gently curving swathes of sand. Sometimes more than one surf club occupies the area, and this is the case with the Manly stretch of beach which accommodates Manly, North Steyne and the Queenscliff Surf Lifesaving Clubs.

As you travel north up the coast, the sand becomes coarser and the colour changes from palest yellow to a warmer red hue, stained by the iron compounds found in the sandstone.

Manly Beach is on the ocean side of an isthmus that joins Manly to North Head.

Aerial view of Dee Why Head and Curl Curl Beach.

Balmoral Beach viewed from Rocky Point.

Barrenjoey Head Lighthouse with Palm Beach to the left and Pittwater to the right.

Looking north from Manly Beach to North Steyne and Queenscliff.

Avalon Beach looking west.

Lifesavers competing in the march-past at a surf carnival, Freshwater Beach.

A surfboat ploughs through the breakers at the start of a race.

A magificent view of the Three Sisters and Jamison Valley.

From Katoomba the Scenic Cableway drops 545 metres into Jamison Valley.

Blue Mountains

paradise unbound

The Blue Mountains are about two hours drive west of Sydney and have been a holiday playground since the railway first went through in the 1880s. Their name comes from the blue haze, which is caused by light reflecting from airborne droplets of eucalyptus oil exuded by the gum tree forests. About 250 000 hectares are a national park and the Greater Blue Mountains area has World Heritage Listing.

Katoomba is a central point in the Blue Mountains. The area's renowned guesthouses, supplemented by hotels and motels, provide accommodation for sightseers, birdwatchers and bushwalkers. Gardeners delight in the beautiful gardens — Leura and Mount Wilson are particularly noteworthy. Here the soil and climate bring exquisite blooms in spring and the magnificent yellows and russet reds of deciduous trees in autumn.

South Coast

seaside cities and retreats

Wollongong (an Aboriginal word meaning "sound of the sea") is 80 kilometres south of Sydney. It is the largest city on the south coast. Just south of Wollongong is Port Kembla, where BHP have built steelworks on an artificially created inner harbour.

The area is backed by the Illawarra Escarpment, site of many of the coal deposits for which the area is famous. The Illawarra coastal plain was an early centre for cedar-harvesting and this was why the original wharf or staithe was built at Wollongong in 1844. The over-exploitation of the timber has led to the virtual extinction of Australian Red Cedar.

The far south coast is now referred to as the Sapphire Coast. It is famed for its beautiful beaches, fishing fleets and dairy industry.

Fishing is an important industry in Wollongong, and Belmore Basin harbours many small fishing vessels along with pleasure craft.

Fitzroy Falls in Morton National Park on the Illawarra Escarpment.

Central Coast

a natural wonderland

The central coast runs roughly from Sydney north to Newcastle and is centred on the city of Gosford. The towns in the Gosford area are located either on the coast or on the shores of Brisbane Water, which is an arm running north from Broken Bay.

Once a holiday resort for Sydney, the central coast has become an area from which residents commute daily on fast, clean electric trains.

Further north from Gosford is The Entrance, the town where Tuggerah Lake meets the sea. West of The Entrance and at the other side of Tuggerah Lake is Wyong, while Budgewoi lies on the north of the lake. There are strong thoroughbred racing clubs at both Gosford and Wyong.

A lone surf fisherman on Frazer Beach, Munmorah State Conservation Area.

From an early age, Steve Parish has been driven by his undying passion for Australia to photograph every aspect of it, from its wild animals and plants to its many wild places. Then he began to turn his camera on Australians and their ways of life. This body of work forms one of Australia's most diverse photographic libraries. Over the years, these images of Australia have been used in thousands of publications, from cards, calendars and stationery to books – pictorial, reference, guide and children's. Steve has combined his considerable talents as a photographer, writer, poet and public speaker with his acute sense of needs in the marketplace to create a publishing company that today is recognised worldwide.

Steve's primary goal is to turn the world on to nature, and, in pursuit of this lifelong objective, he has published a world-class range of children's books and learning aids. He sees our children as the decision makers of tomorrow and the guardians of our heritage.

Published by Steve Parish Publishing Pty Ltd
PO Box 1058, Archerfield, Queensland 4108 Australia

ISBN 978174021085 0
First published 2001. Reprinted 2003, 2004, 2005 (twice), 2006, 2007, 2008, 2010 (twice).
Photography and text: Steve Parish
Photographic assistance: Phillip Hayson; Emma Harm, SPP
Additional photography: pp. 18–19 (centre), courtesy of Sydney Wildlife World; p. 25 (right), David Messent, Photolibrary.com

Design: Leanne Nobilio, SPP
Editorial: Ted Lewis; Michele Perry & Karin Cox, SPP
Production: Tiffany Johnson

Cover: Sydney Opera House; Sydney Harbour Bridge (inset). Title page: Sydney Harbour Bridge. pp. 2–3: Sydney vista looking west from the Heads. pp. 4–5: Sydney vista looking south from North Sydney. pp. 62–63: Putty Beach, Bouddi National Park and Broken Bay. Back cover: Sydney Harbour Bridge and Opera House.

Prepress by Colour Chiefs Digital Imaging, Brisbane, Australia
Printed and bound in China by 1010 Printing International Ltd

Produced in Australia at the Steve Parish Publishing Studios

SP PUBLISHING

www.steveparish.com.au
www.photographaustralia.com.au